RAISING GORDY GORILLA AT THE SAN DIEGO ZOO

ZOO WORLD

RAISING

GORDY GORILLA

AT THE SAN DIEGO ZOO

BY GEORGEANNE IRVINE

SIMON AND SCHUSTER BOOKS FOR YOUNG READERS
Published by Simon & Schuster Inc, New York

ACKNOWLEDGMENTS

My special thanks and appreciation to: JoAnn Thomas-Roemer, Peggy Sexton, Ron Garrison, Janet Hawes, Ken Kelley, Craig Racicot, Alison Holland, Gale Foland, Joe Kalla, Phil Ensley, Carlee Robinson, Dorothy Irvine, Victoria Garrison and Susanne Abildgaard for their support, enthusiasm, and assistance with Gordy's story.

PHOTO CREDITS

Ron Garrison: front and back covers, endsheets; 5; 6; 9; 13; 14 right; 15 left; 17 lower; 20; 21; 22; 23; 24; 32; 33; 34; 35; 36; 37; 38; 39; 40; 41. Susanne Abildgaard: 44. Phil Ensley: 14 left. Janet Hawes: 15 right; 16; 17 top. Georgeanne Irvine: 26 top left; 42. Ken Kelley: 10; 12; 28; 29; 30; 31. Craig Racicot: 18; 19; 25; 26 lower left and right; 27.

SIMON AND SCHUSTER
BOOKS FOR YOUNG READERS
Simon & Schuster Building
Rockefeller Center
1230 Avenue of the Americas
New York, New York 10020
Text and photos copyright © 1990 by Zoological Society
of San Diego and Georgeanne Irvine
SIMON AND SCHUSTER BOOKS FOR YOUNG READERS
is a trademark of Simon & Schuster Inc.
Manufactured in the United States of America
10 9 8 7 6 5 4 3 2 1

Library of Congress Cataloging-in-Publication Data
Irvine, Georgeanne.
Raising Gordy gorilla at the San Diego Zoo.
Includes bibliographical references.
Summary: Describes the early years in the life of
a gorilla born in captivity at the San Diego Zoo
and later moved to the San Diego Wild Animal Park.
1. Gorillas—Juvenile literature.
[1. Gorillas.]   I. Title.
QL737.P96I784   1990
599.88'46—dc20   89-35735
AC
ISBN 0-671-68775-1
Designed by Kathleen Westray

To Gordy Gorilla,
who will always hold a special place in my heart,
and to Carole Seaton for giving me a chance and for
inspiring and encouraging me over the years.

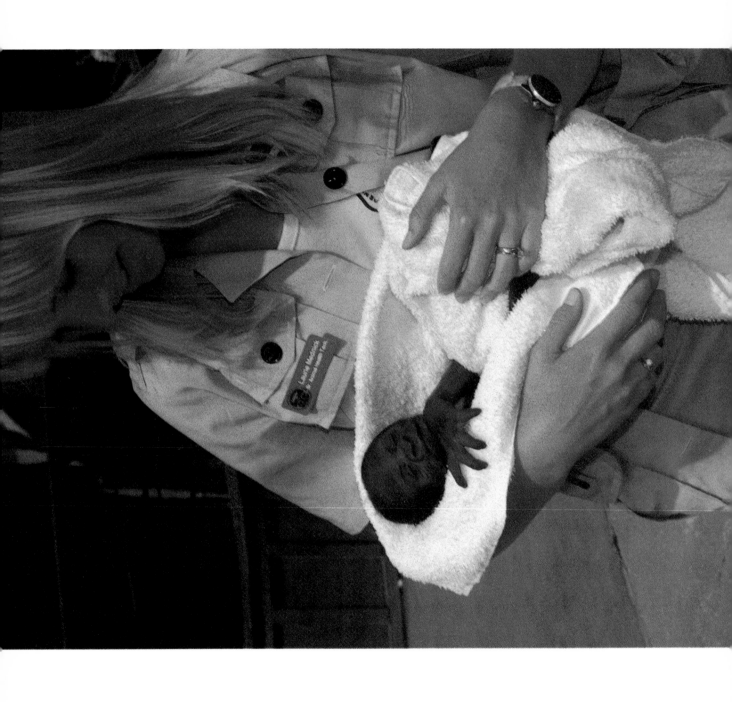

IT WAS THE FIRST DAY of May, a time to celebrate spring and new life. But the baby gorilla who was rushed to the San Diego Zoo's nursery would die if he didn't eat soon.

Gordy Gorilla had arrived a whole month early. His mother, Alvila, was expecting him in late May of 1986. What a surprise it was when the keepers found Alvila cradling a 3¼-pound baby boy in her arms on the morning of April 29.

Gordy was a special baby because he was only the second gorilla ever born at the San Diego Zoo. Alvila had been the first, more than twenty years earlier. Gordy's father, Memba, was a 400-pound silverback who had arrived in San Diego from an English zoo in 1985. He was born in the jungles of Africa.

Alvila was a good mother. She held little Gordy close to her to keep him warm, and licked him so he would be clean. She seemed proud of her new son, and sat next to the bars of her sleeping room so the keepers could see infant Gordy up close.

But something was wrong. Gordy wouldn't nurse from his mother. The keepers took turns watching him round-the-clock to make sure he was healthy and eating well. But not once during Gordy's first two days of life did he swallow even a drop of his mother's milk.

The zoo veterinarian was concerned. He put Alvila to sleep with a drug. He took the newborn baby from her, wrapping him in a towel. Then the vet's truck rushed Gordy to the nursery. There, human attendants would try to get the hungry infant ape to eat.

The plan was to return Gordy to Alvila in a few days, when he was stronger and had milk in his tummy. It is better for a mother gorilla to raise her own baby. Families are very important to the gorilla way of life.

When Gordy arrived at the nursery, he was so weak he couldn't open his eyes. Attendant JoAnn Thomas-Roemer tried to feed him a milk formula from a bottle. As hungry as Gordy was, he couldn't suck milk on his own. The veterinarian figured that he hadn't developed the ability to suck milk yet because he had been born a month early.

JoAnn held her fingers around the corners of Gordy's mouth and under his chin to help him grab hold of the nipple of the feeding bottle. Now, with JoAnn's help, Gordy was able to drink. Every two hours, when it was time for more milk, JoAnn helped his tiny gorilla lips grasp the nipple.

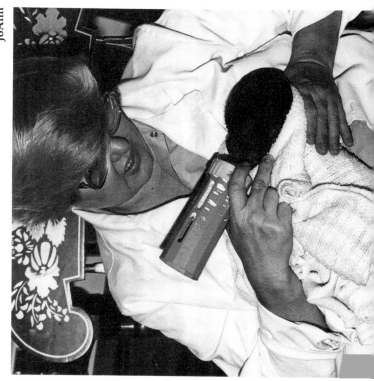

JoAnn

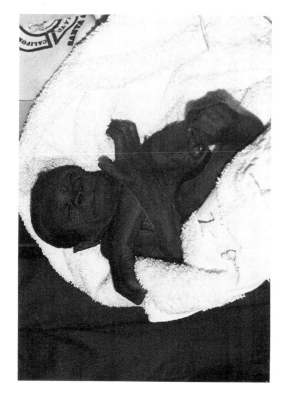

Gordy slept in an incubator to keep his fragile body warm. He was dressed in a nightshirt for warmth, too, and wore diapers to stay clean. The weak baby gorilla lay very still in his bed.

When JoAnn went home for the day, other nursery attendants came to baby-sit Gordy. They fed him and cared for him all through the night.

Gordy grew stronger over the next couple of days. He opened his eyes and even moved around a bit. The zoo veterinarian said he could go back to Alvila. The vet hoped Gordy would nurse on his own.

Early on a Sunday morning, when Gordy was six days old, Alvila was once again put to sleep. The veterinarian and keepers carried Gordy to her. They watched and waited, hoping he would nurse from his mother. Although he was very hungry because he had missed his morning bottle, Gordy just couldn't drink a drop of his mother's milk.

The only way to keep Gordy alive was to take him back to the nursery. JoAnn and the other attendants would make sure he got plenty of milk in his belly. He would be raised by the nursery attendants until he was a year old, when he'd learn to live with other gorillas.

JoAnn was thrilled to be looking after cute baby Gordy. She had cared for Alvila when she was young. Watching Alvila's son grow would be a treat for JoAnn.

In the beginning, Gordy was the quietest ape the nursery attendants had ever raised. The pygmy chimpanzees and orangutans they cared for were much more playful at an early age.

When he got older and stronger, Gordy was moved from the incubator to a wooden crib. Warm, fuzzy blankets, soft pillows, and furry toy animals surrounded him. Gordy's blankets were important to him. He hugged them for security.

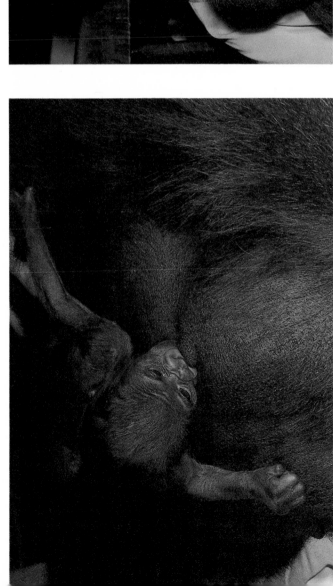

If he had stayed with his mother, he would have clung to her for security, just as all baby gorillas do.

As the weeks passed, it became easier and easier for Gordy to drink milk on his own. But milk wasn't his only food for long. Like a human baby, this gorilla kid learned to eat baby food! When he was a month and a half old, Gordy ate his first spoonful of Gerber's strained vegetables. Yum! It was fun to have something new, and he gobbled it up. Two weeks later came strained fruit. That was even tastier. The fruit soon became Gordy's favorite food—but he was treated to it only after he finished his vegetables!

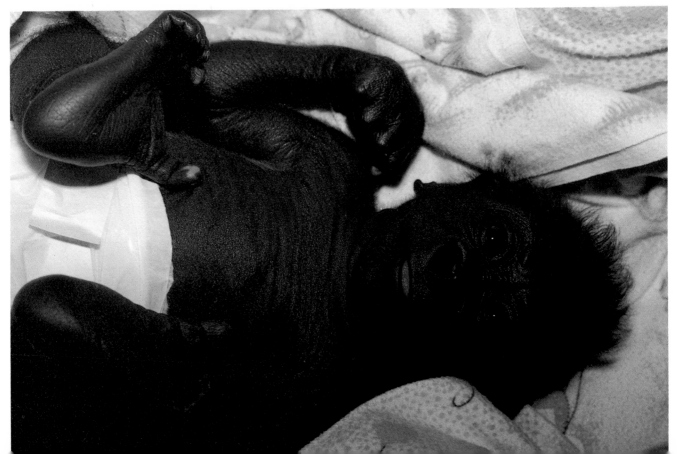

One day, quiet Gordy was very cranky. His temperature was high, but the nursery attendants weren't worried. Gordy was teething. By August he had two front teeth!

When he was four months old, the infant gorilla could sit up by himself. He was a little wobbly at first, but that's how all babies are. He rolled from his back to his stomach, too. Then, a week after he first sat up, mild-mannered Gordy grabbed the side of his crib with his chubby fingers and pulled himself up. Gordy could stand! He was pleased and giggled to himself. A baby gorilla's giggles are happy, chuckly sounds.

For San Diego Zoo visitors, nothing was more fun than watching a baby gorilla. Gordy's crib was right next to the nursery window. People smiled as he played with his rattles and toys. Gordy enjoyed looking back at them. There were so many colors and faces to study!

The day he climbed up and hung over the side of his crib, visitors laughed and laughed. Gordy was behaving like an acrobat. But the nursery attendants didn't think the little ape was funny at all. They were worried that he might fall and hurt himself. It was time to move growing Gordy Gorilla into a big wire pen with a top on it.

His new home had plastic chains for climbing, a tire hanging from a rope for swinging…and a thick, padded floor for tumbling. Toys and blankets were everywhere. A young ape could get plenty of exercise in this pen.

Gordy raced around and around his new home. He swung from his tire. He laughed because he was having such a good time. Then he climbed all the way to the top of the pen. He looked at nursery attendant Alison, and cried and cried. Gordy couldn't get down!

Alison rushed to the rescue. Gordy wasn't really stuck. He was just scared. He had never climbed that high before. Alison hugged and talked to the little gorilla to comfort him. Her voice was soothing. The next time Gordy climbed to the top of his pen, he scrambled back down with ease.

17

Alison

Gordy was getting bigger now. At six months of age, he weighed almost eleven pounds, and he could eat chunks of fruit and vegetables instead of baby food. Apples and oranges were fine, but bananas were Gordy's favorite snack. He also munched on high-protein biscuits called monkey chow.

A television producer called the zoo. Gordy and the zoo's goodwill ambassador, Joan Embery, were invited to appear on "The Tonight Show." Joan would talk to the show's host, Johnny Carson, about Gordy and teach the TV viewers about gorillas.

Gordy was a healthy eight-month-old, and the zoo veterinarians said he could make the trip to Los Angeles to tape the show. Nursery attendants JoAnn and Janet went along to care for him. They drove 135 miles to Los Angeles in a zoo van. Gordy played with JoAnn the whole way there. When they arrived at the studio, he climbed into Janet's lap.

The dressing room at the studio was even more fun. It had two stars on the door. One read JOAN EMBERY, and the other GORDY GORILLA. Gordy had many toys to play with, but he was more interested in paper cups and cuddling his nursery attendants.

The best thing about the room was the big

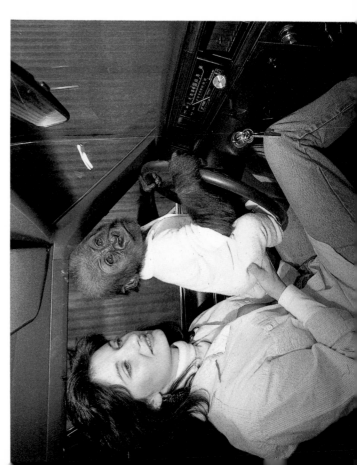

mirror that stretched from the floor to the ceiling. Gordy had never seen a mirror before. And he'd never ever seen a young gorilla!

When he looked in the mirror, he saw a little gorilla staring back at him. Gordy ran up to the mirror, smacked it, and ran away. He peeked at the mirror again. The little gorilla peeked back at him.

Gordy puffed out his chest like big gorillas do. He ran sideways back and forth in front of the

mirror, looking out of the corners of his eyes. The other little gorilla did the same. JoAnn and Janet laughed out loud. Gordy began to relax. He realized that the mirror gorilla wouldn't hurt him.

Johnny Carson loved Gordy Gorilla. While Joan Embery talked about Gordy, he climbed into Johnny's arms. The audience laughed because Johnny tried to feed Gordy a banana. Instead of eating it, Gordy let the banana chunk hang out of his mouth.

Gordy had other adventures, too. One big adventure happened right in the nursery whenever he took a bath.

Bathtime was playtime for Gordy. He loved sitting in the nursery sink while water rained on his head from the spigot. Catching water in his mouth made Gordy giggle and laugh. He closed his eyes so he wouldn't get soap in them, even though it was the kind of soap that didn't sting. JoAnn was the only nursery attendant whom Gordy would let bathe him. He was always wild

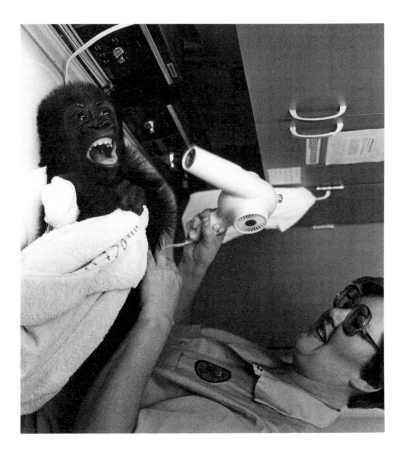

and wiggly with the others. He'd grab the shampoo bottle and knock it over. Then he'd twist and turn in the sink, sliding all around. And if a nursery attendant turned for even a second, Gordy climbed right out of the sink!

To dry the baby gorilla, JoAnn rubbed him with a soft, fluffy towel. The hair dryer was next. Gordy liked the warm and breezy air from the hair dryer. Finally, JoAnn patted Gordy with mineral oil so his skin wouldn't dry out. How handsome he looked!

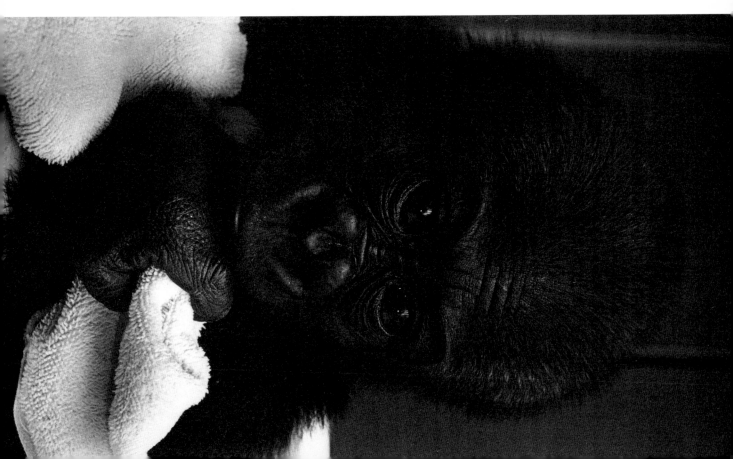

The older Gordy got, the more playful he became. He was nothing like the quiet baby gorilla who had arrived at the nursery wrapped in a towel. He was a rough-and-tumble young gorilla now.

Often, the nursery attendants let Gordy out of his wire pen to play in the nursery. They worked in the same room with him while he played by himself. They always kept an eye on him, though. You never know when a young gorilla might get into trouble.

Gordy climbed on everything: the dressers,

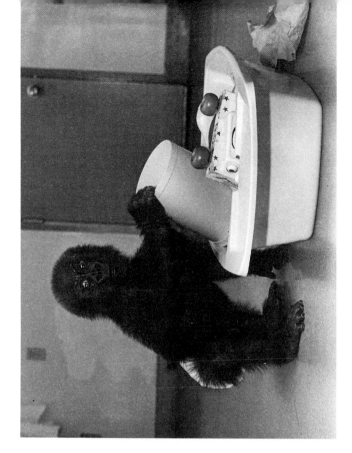

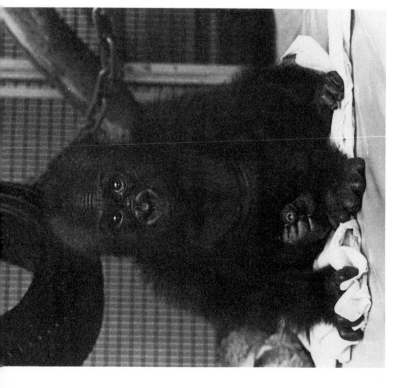

the cribs, even the incubators. He roamed around the room, exploring every corner of the nursery. He liked peering into the pens of the other nursery animals. He was allowed to watch but not touch them.

If Gordy got too wild, pulling pots and pans out of the cupboards or tipping a trash can, he was

sent to his pen for a while. Gordy was smart enough to know when he was getting into mischief—but it was fun, anyway!

As a special treat, Gordy was allowed to ride piggyback on his nursery attendants. It was more difficult for them to get their work done, but they knew Gordy enjoyed the ride.

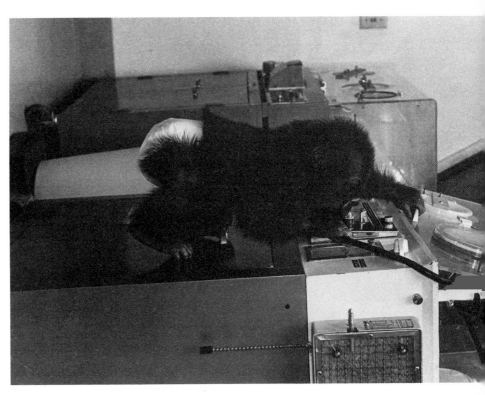

Roughhousing was Gordy's favorite activity. Young gorillas are very strong and sturdy. It is healthy for them to be rowdy. Gordy loved JoAnn to grab hold of his arms and swing him up and down, back and forth. The higher she'd swing him, the happier he was. Because gorilla bodies are built for swinging, this kind of play was good exercise for Gordy.

Spinning was another favorite Gordy-game. When he wanted to play, he lay on his back by his nursery attendant's feet. She'd bend down and spin him like a top. He giggled as he went round and round. After a spin, his nursery attendant slid Gordy on his behind a few feet across the slick floor. Gordy ran back for more spinning and sliding. When he had had enough, he sat down to rest.

Sometimes, when Gordy was out playing, he needed a hug. Like human children, it was important for him to know he was loved. Gordy had his own ways of telling his nursery attendants he wanted extra attention. If they were sitting down, he climbed into their laps. If they were standing up, he'd cling to their legs. And if he was in his pen, he sucked his thumb or whimpered to get their attention.

The nursery attendants loved Gordy dearly. But he was nearly a year old, and it would soon be

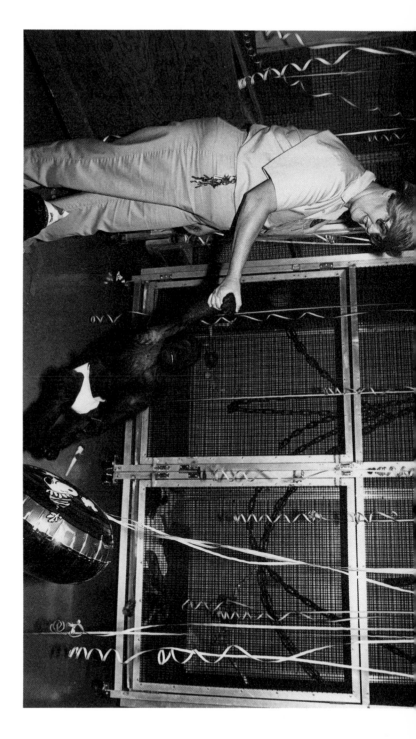

time for him to leave the nursery and live with other gorillas.

On April 29, Gordy's first birthday, the nursery looked different than it ever had before. All of the cribs and pens had been pushed against the wall to make room for a little table in the center of the room. The table was stacked high with presents. Colorful balloons and streamers hung from the ceiling. A sign that read PARTY ANIMAL was posted nearby. The nursery attendants were throwing a birthday party for Gordy.

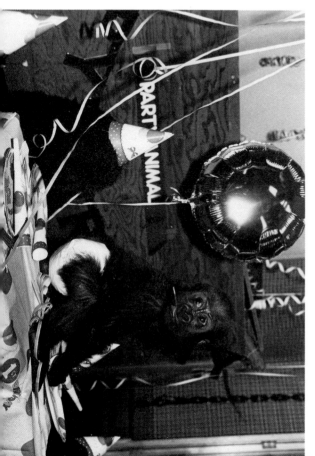

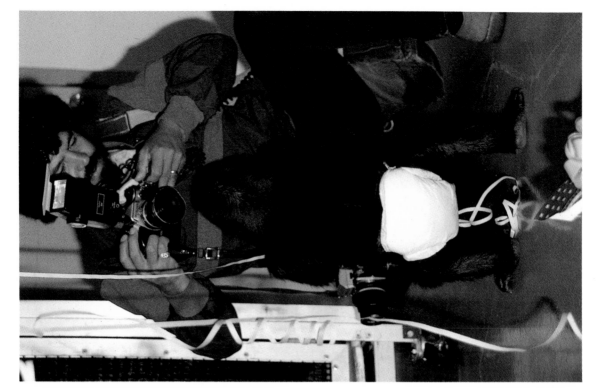

JoAnn, Gordy, and Kathi Diamant

Early that morning, several hours before his party began, JoAnn took Gordy to a local television talk show. She told all of the viewers that it was his first birthday, and she invited them to the zoo to watch him celebrate. They could peek at him through the nursery windows. Kathi Diamant, the talk show host, gave Gordy a birthday present to open on the air. But Gordy didn't seem to care much about the gift: he was too busy drinking milk from his bottle.

Gordy's party was a fine affair. His guests were furry toy gorillas wearing party hats. The streamers were fun to pull as they dangled from the ceiling. Gordy batted at the balloons as if they were punching bags. But the cake covered with whipped cream and fresh fruit didn't interest Gordy at all. He kissed the frosting, but then sat down to chew on a birthday horn instead.

Gordy had the most fun with the newspaper and television people who came to do stories about his birthday. He climbed all over the reporters. The photographers had a tough time taking his picture because he wanted to play with their cameras. Even so, that night, people all over San Diego saw Gordy's picture in the newspaper. They watched him pull the streamers, chew on the horn, and kiss his cake on the television news.

The following week, the plans began for Gordy's move. At last he was strong, healthy, and old enough to leave the nursery. He was ready to learn to live with other gorillas.

The zookeepers thought about reintroducing Gordy to his mother, Alvila, and his father, Memba, who lived at the zoo. They decided, however, that Gordy would be happier living at the San Diego Wild Animal Park. The park is a wildlife preserve where animals like giraffes, zebras, gazelles, and rhinoceroses live together in large open enclosures similar to their homes in the wild. There, he would have another young gorilla his own age as a playmate. He could live with a whole group, or troop, of gorillas. Gorillas in the jungles of Africa live in troops.

Leaving the San Diego Zoo meant a major change in Gordy's life. There wouldn't be any more nursery toys or birthday parties or trips to television shows. Living with a real gorilla family, though, was what the zookeepers knew was best for Gordy.

On Gordy's last morning in the zoo nursery, JoAnn packed a small bag for him. In it were Gordy's favorite blankets and a few feeding bottles. JoAnn was to take Gordy to meet his new Wild Animal Park keepers—and his new gorilla family.

Some zoo friends sent a long, blue limousine to take Gordy and JoAnn the thirty miles to the park. The limousine drove right up to the nursery. A chauffeur dressed in a dark suit opened the car door for the special passengers.

The limousine was a great place for Gordy to explore. He turned on the television, then banged on the screen. Gordy grabbed the telephone and held it up to his mouth. He inspected the drinking glasses, probably hoping there was a drop of milk in them. He swung from the ceiling of the limousine, and peeked out of the window, watching the other cars go by on the freeway.

A ranger greeted JoAnn and Gordy at the Wild Animal Park's back entrance. Everybody at the park knew Gordy was coming. The ranger shook his hand through the window, and said the keepers were waiting to meet him at the gorilla exhibit. The limousine drove right through the Wild Animal Park, and stopped next to Gordy's new home.

Gordy reached from JoAnn into gorilla keeper Peggy Sexton's arms for a hello hug. He was a little scared because this new place was strange and different. There were unusual sights, sounds, and smells. The other keepers gathered around Peggy to admire the new gorilla.

29

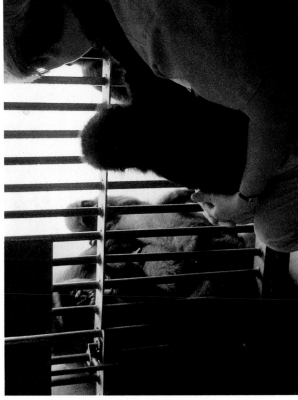

It would take time for Gordy to get used to his new surroundings and new family. There were many gorillas to get to know. Trib, a 450-pound silverback, was the leader of the family. Three adult females—Dolly, Vila, and Kami—would take care of Gordy. A 7-year-old male, Jitu, would be a rowdy "big brother" for the little zoo gorilla. And, best of all, 1½-year-old Schroeder was the perfect gorilla playmate for him. They were just about the same size!

Together with JoAnn and the park gorilla keepers, Gordy took his first look at his new family. JoAnn sat with Gordy in a hallway that was separated from the outside gorilla exhibit by bars. Gordy clutched his blanket while the gorillas gathered on the other side of the bars to see him. They were very interested in Gordy.

Little Schroeder reached through the bars and touched Gordy lightly on the head. Schroeder had never seen another young gorilla before. Trib, who is big but gentle, stretched a finger toward Gordy. More curious than scared, Gordy touched back. Gordy's tiny hand was no larger than one of Trib's enormous fingers.

Before JoAnn said good-bye, she held Gordy in her arms one last time. She was sad because she would no longer be seeing Gordy every day, but she was pleased that he would have a real gorilla family to care for him. She knew he would be happiest with his own kind.

The park keepers planned to make Gordy's introductions go as smoothly as possible. Because he was the new kid on the block, he was to meet only a few gorillas at a time. That way he wouldn't be overwhelmed with too many gorillas at once.

For the next few weeks, Gordy stayed indoors in the gorilla sleeping area getting to know Schroeder, Dolly, and Vila. They lived in several adjoining rooms. One room had a door open only wide enough for Gordy and Schroeder to squeeze through. This was so Gordy could get away from Dolly and Vila if he felt shy or scared.

The gorilla keepers took turns watching Gordy and the other gorillas twenty-four hours a day. Gordy stayed in the front of his room near the keepers, and as far from the other gorillas as possible. It was comforting for Gordy to know that a human friend was nearby, and he whimpered if the keeper left the area for even a few minutes. He clung to the blanket he had brought from the nursery because it was familiar to him.

Schroeder became Gordy's first gorilla friend. They started out playing tag and chase. Although Gordy wasn't used to gorilla games, in a short time he and Schroeder were wrestling and tumbling together.

Gordy stayed away from Dolly and Vila in his private room, clutching his blanket while he watched Schroeder play with them. Schroeder wasn't shy: Dolly was his mother, and Vila had been around since he was born.

One day, Vila reached her long arm through the door of Gordy's private room and grabbed his blanket. She waggled the blanket in the doorway, probably hoping Gordy would come after it.

Gordy wanted his blanket back. He sat for a while staring at Vila. Finally, he scurried to her side to claim the beloved blanket. Gordy stayed in the room with Vila for several minutes. Dolly and Schroeder were there, too. Slowly, they were becoming a family.

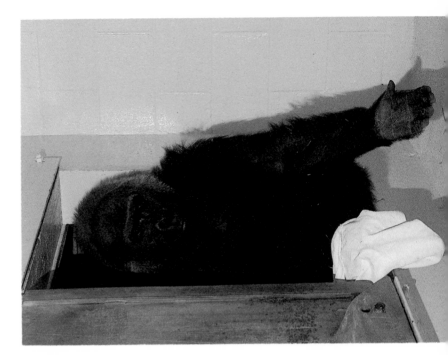

Vila

Gordy (left) and Schroeder

Only three weeks had passed since Gordy's arrival at the Wild Animal Park. He was adjusting to life with the gorillas faster than the keepers had expected. The time had come for Gordy to visit the outside gorilla exhibit.

Outside, Gordy played on grass for the first time ever. There were logs for climbing and trees for shade. A stream gurgled through the center of the enclosure, emptying into a pond. A grassy hillside was a great place from which the gorillas could look down on the Wild Animal Park visitors.

Schroeder helps Gordy up.

Gordy's first day in his new outside home was a bit rough. He climbed to the top of the grassy hillside and couldn't get down. Just like the time he had climbed to the top of his nursery pen, he was afraid. Dolly and Vila scrambled up after him, so he could follow them down the hill. And after he whimpered a bit, Gordy discovered that heading downhill was easy.

When Gordy went to bed that night, he looked a little pink. He was sunburned! He had never been out in the sun for such a long time.

The veterinarian said Gordy would be fine. He'd get used to the sun.

Schroeder on Vila's back, Gordy, and Dolly

A few weeks later, Gordy met Kami, the third adult female in the gorilla troop. She was excited at meeting Gordy...and he was enchanted with her. There was an instant bonding and friendship between them. Kami would become Gordy's adopted mother. Their relationship was like the one he would have had if he'd been raised by his mother, Alvila. Gordy stayed by Kami's side, rode piggyback on her, and cuddled with her. They spent lots of time in the gorilla enclosure together. Gordy still played with Dolly, Vila, and Schroeder, but Kami became his closest friend.

Gordy and Kami

Finally, Gordy met rowdy Jitu and the head of the gorilla troop, big Trib. Like a good big brother, Jitu coaxed Gordy up on his back for piggyback rides. He wrestled with Gordy, too. Rough-and-tumble play was fun and healthy for Jitu, Gordy, and Schroeder.

Even though Trib was more than twenty times bigger than Gordy, he played with the little fellow. Trib was a gentle gorilla father. Gordy liked to sneak up behind Trib and swat him on the legs. Then he would run away. Trib didn't mind at all. Trib also made sure the other gorillas behaved themselves around Gordy. If Jitu played too rough, one stern glance from Trib stopped any kind of gorilla mischief.

Gordy and Jitu

Trib

Schroeder, Vila, and Gordy

Gordy was the youngest gorilla at the Wild Animal Park. People who had watched him growing up at the zoo could visit him at the park. They saw Gordy exploring, wrestling, and playing with his new family. Sometimes, he sunbathed in a pile of leaves. Or he played hide-and-seek with Jitu and Schroeder behind a tree stump. Gordy acted silly, too, making funny faces or sticking his foot in his mouth, and learned to thump on his chest like big gorillas do. When he got tired of playing, Gordy always snuggled up to Kami.

When Gordy was $2\frac{1}{2}$ years old, something special and unusual happened: Kami gave birth to a baby. Trib, the baby's father, had a new gorilla in his troop. The infant was given the name Paul Donn. Paul Donn's birth was special because gorilla births in captivity are rare.

Gordy didn't know what to do about Paul Donn. He had never seen a newborn gorilla before. That first day, Kami couldn't pay attention to Gordy because she was busy caring for Paul Donn. Gordy was jealous, and stayed away from Kami and her infant. Jitu, who seemed to sense Gordy was feeling bad, gave him plenty of attention. That helped a little, but Gordy began to miss Kami.

The next day, Gordy snuggled up to Kami. While she held Paul Donn in one arm, Kami cuddled Gordy with the other. The three of them took naps together. Having a new gorilla around wasn't so bad for Gordy after all.

Gordy was no longer the littlest gorilla in the troop. But that didn't seem to matter. It was Gordy's turn to be a big brother to Paul Donn. Someday, they'd wrestle together, play hide-and-seek, and romp up the hillside just as Gordy did with Schroeder and Jitu. Now Gordy could join the other gorillas in teaching baby Paul Donn about life in a big gorilla family.

Kami and Paul Donn

Kami, Paul Donn, and Gordy

mountain gorilla

I N CENTRAL AFRICA, where the forests are thick with lush leafy plants and dotted with open green meadows, lives the biggest and the gentlest of the great apes: the gorilla.

Years ago, people thought gorillas were mean and nasty-tempered, but the opposite is true. Gorillas are quiet, intelligent animals that lead calm lives when left alone. Nicknamed "gentle giants," gorillas are peaceful yet powerful, shy yet sociable.

Gorillas live in family groups called "troops." The leader of the troop is a large adult male, called a "silverback" because the hair on his back is a sil-very-white color. Also living in the troop are adult females and their babies, young males called "blackbacks," and juveniles. Between five and thirty gorillas live in a troop.

If a silverback's troop is in danger, he will per-form a furious display to frighten intruders away. He screams and hoots, charges through the forest, breaks branches, and beats on his chest. Only rarely does the silverback need to fight to protect his family.

Most of a gorilla's day is spent foraging for food. Because gorillas are vegetarians, the forest is like a salad to them, filled with delicious leaves, shoots, stems, barks, grasses, and vines. The gentle giants also like wild celery, thistles, and banana leaves. Fruit is a special treat when they can find it.

At night, gorillas sleep in nests they build for themselves by trampling plants. Sometimes, they make nests in the forks of trees, several feet off the ground.

Gorillas communicate with each other through gestures, body movement, facial expressions, and sometimes by making sounds.

Three different types, or "subspecies," of gorilla live in Africa. *Western lowland gorillas* live in the hot forests of western central Africa. Gordy and his family are this type of gorilla. *Eastern lowland gorillas* come from the lower forests of central Africa, and *mountain gorillas* live where the weather gets very cold, high up in the Virunga Mountains of central Africa.

All gorillas are "endangered," which means they will become extinct some day unless people do everything possible to save them. They're endangered because poachers have killed them for food and to make souvenirs out of their body parts, and because people have cut down their forest homes for farmland and lumber.

Zoos around the world are trying to help save gorillas by educating people about how special they are, and by breeding them in captivity. Governments in Africa have set aside forest preserves for gorillas and are working hard to stop poachers from killing them.

mountain gorilla

44

BIBLIOGRAPHY

Fenner, Carol, *Gorilla, Gorilla*. New York: Random House, 1973.

Fossey, Dian, *Gorillas in the Mist*. Boston: Houghton Mifflin Company, 1983.

Groves, Colin P., *The World of Animals: Gorillas*. New York: Arco Publishing Company, 1970.

Kevles, Betty Ann, *Thinking Gorillas*. New York: E.P. Dutton, 1980.

McClung, Robert M., *Gorilla*. New York: William Morrow and Company, 1984.

McDearmon, Kay, *Gorillas*. New York: Dodd, Mead & Company, 1979.

Patterson, Dr. Francine, *Koko's Kitten*. New York: Scholastic, Inc., 1985.

———, *Koko's Story*. New York: Scholastic, Inc., 1987.

Wexo, John Bonnett, *Zoobooks: Gorillas*. San Diego: Wildlife Education Ltd., 1984.

VIDEOS

Gorilla, produced by The National Geographic Society, 1981. 60 minutes. An informative, in-depth look at the mountain gorillas of central Africa.

San Diego Zoo: It's a Wild Life! produced by VideoTours and the San Diego Zoo, 1986. 30 minutes. A behind-the-scenes look at the San Diego Zoo, featuring film of Gordy in the nursery.

Gorillas in the Mist, produced by Arnold Glimcher and Terrence Clegg, 1988. 129 minutes. A feature-length movie about the life of Dian Fossey and her work studying and protecting wild mountain gorillas in Africa.